First Responder Chaplains

First Responder Chaplains

Spiritual Caregivers

D R . L A R R Y B E N N E T T

ISBN: 1535236337
ISBN 13: 9781535236331
Library of Congress Control Number: 2016913286
CreateSpace Independent Publishing Platform
North Charleston, South Carolina

Contents

Introduction

"The average believer lives as an enemy of the cross — refusing its demands, but expecting to enjoy its privileges".

- DAVID RAVENHILL

In recent years there has been a new emphasis on the development of what is known as "first responder chaplains." These people are being trained by different churches, denominations and faith based organizations on the importance of being available to respond in the event of a local, state, or national disaster. These disasters include storms, hurricanes, tornados, earthquakes, and other events that need trained individuals in the time of need.

Though there is a need for such training and exposing interested volunteers on how they can respond and help during a disaster however this training does not give the volunteer the expert training or specialized training they need to be classified as a law enforcement chaplain, fire/rescue chaplain, hospital chaplain or hospice chaplain. These chaplains serve in specialized ministries and over the years have gone through specialized training to serve in that capacity.

The intention of this book is not to discourage individuals who are interested in serving their faith based ministry as a volunteer, but to distinguish the difference between a volunteer who wants to serve in the time of a disaster and those chaplains who have received specialized training.

A "first responder" chaplain is exactly what it says; it is a chaplain who has received specialized training and is certified to ride in a police car or a fire/rescue vehicle and is the first to respond with the emergency personnel. When a chaplain is called to the scene of an emergency they have gained the respect of their department and their department has called them to the scene to assist as a chaplain in whatever way the personnel deems necessary.

Those trained as volunteers should not identify themselves as chaplains within their community because the only time that they are going to be called on is when their denomination asks them to respond to a disaster as a representative of their denomination. Usually that response is going to be in another state. When these individuals identity as a "first responder chaplain" within a community it causes identification problems within law enforcement, fire/rescue, hospital and hospice personnel.

Why is there so much boredom, restlessness, and unfulfillment in the world today? I believe that the problem is found in the fact that many people have no sense of vision, no understanding of God's divine purpose for their lives.

The Apostle Paul asks an important question in Acts 9:6; *"What shall I do Lord?"* The Lord answered, *"Arise, and go into Damascus and there you will be told of all that I have appointed for you to do."* The word *Lord* implies submission. The command, *Go into Damascus,"* designates location. The instructions, *And there you will be told of all that has been appointed for you to do,"* indicates vocation.

One

The Theology of Chaplaincy

Missions and the mission field are buss words that flow out of every church. Many churches are strong mission minded and they spend an inordinate amount of time raising mission funds. The mission field as we know it is basically sending ministers to foreign countries to tell people the message of Jesus Christ. But missions have many places where people can serve. One of those mission fields is chaplaincy within the community to law enforcement and fire/rescue agencies which can be part of the Great Commission (Matthew 28:18, 19). To serve as a chaplain in this mission field an individual must have a calling and a desire for this type of ministry. The ministry is bright and accessible through proper training and understanding what is expected by the individual candidate. However it is not recommended that the individual wanting to serve as a chaplain within the community be a lead pastor of a local congregation. That congregation will always be the focus and primary calling of the pastor and he will not be able to give adequate time to serving as a chaplain.

The marketplace is so ripe for missions that there are now over 1400 corporate chaplains in the USA alone and that does not include chaplains. Most Christian training centers and Bible Colleges that are producing Christian missionaries only see the mission field as in some foreign country where people have never heard the gospel. Yet there is a vast mission field here in the United States known as the marketplace which includes chaplaincy. This demands that the Church re-think her approach to world missions and how she trains future individuals for ministry.

The integration of chaplains into the marketplace requires a theology for marketplace chaplains. This theology must include instruction on how the Word, the Church, and chaplaincy relate, complement, and integrate into the lives of those the chaplain will be serving. A clear concept of theology will greatly affect the training, equipping and deployment of future chaplains. Failure to understand twenty-first century technology, training, and philosophy of the needs of first responders will leave many ill-equipped and the local law enforcement/fire rescue departments that need chaplains will go untouched.

Developing a theology for chaplains does not mean that we abandon our past or discount present methods that still work well. Rather it means that chaplains of the present must not allow the lack of understanding to shut off any expansion of thought, curriculum, and training demanded by twenty - first - century realities.

The local church must see herself as an extension of every household within the church, and that each household is profoundly relational. Gilbert Bilezikian says, "The passion for community is contagious. Our innate need for community is so intense that once a spark of interest is ignited and a glimpse of God's dream for community is captured, a burning passion for community can spread like a wildfire." The Church as a community is indispensible for proper spiritual formation and development. The Church that is living as a family will produce transformation in its members and the members will see the community around them as a mission field.

Chaplaincy in the Marketplace Demands a Strategy

First, The Church must understand that there is a mission field within their city that is just as important as sending missionaries to a foreign country. The Church must have as her goal the fulfillment of the Great Commission (Matthew 28:18, 19) which will help bring transformation to the community. Properly trained and equipped marketplace ministers, known as chaplains, will be part of making this a reality.

The church must see chaplains as part of their mission program and take it upon themselves to support these chaplains from their mission budget, but more importantly the church must support the chaplain with prayer and encouragement.

John W. Kennedy once said, "A scattered pile of bricks is not a house, although they may be united in appearance; one brick looks very much like another. Similarly, a scattered company of people, all claiming that they are in Christ is not a church. They must be 'fitly formed together', each one contributing to his particular place in the spiritual building, and a conscious of the bond of life and actual responsibility which then binds all of them together."

Second is contextualization of the gospel in the marketplace. Contextualization is making Jesus relevant within a culture that needs Him. The culture that chaplains serve is steeped in tradition, non-religious values and a multi-culture. A multi-culture of different ethnic groups, religions and religious philosophies that must be attended to but in a delicate, sensitive, and patient way. Simply put it means being trained to understand the context of realities where you are trying to share the gospel message. It requires an individual to separate himself from all the religious rhetoric and become a purist only serving in a "ministry of presence". It should never mean compromising the message but rather delivering it in such a way that those you are ministering to understand the love of Jesus without restrictions. In this context ministry brings relevance to the need of the individual that you are ministering to. For this reason the Church has invited the world to come to them, but Jesus said, "Go into all the world"(Mark 16:15, 16).

Third, chaplains must have a simple, clear, and comprehensive biblical theology for missions in the marketplace. This theology cannot carry with it all the trappings of the denomination nor the theological sounds of religion. This demands a strong and relevant spiritual character of the individual who is planning to serve as a chaplain. Training for those who are going to serve as chaplains requires a biblical understanding of contemporary marketplace issues as it relates to the professionalism of the department that they are serving. Training requires subject matter that is not theological in nature but rather conducive to the area of missions that the chaplain will be serving. Serving as a chaplain requires training in how that ministry is a "ministry of presence" which is where the chaplain represents Christ, not the Church though the chaplain has been endorsed by the church.

Chaplains must learn to listen and not talk. One of the reasons most pastors do not make good chaplains is because they have a need to talk and be heard. They have a tendency to be preachy rather than a listener. A good chaplain must learn to listen and not be critical or judgmental of the person doing the talking. A chaplain will see and hear things that must not shake him from his biblical foundation nor cause him to become a speaker for the lost. Chaplains must be familiar with subjects that relate to his/her ministry as a chaplain. Such subjects may include mental health, marriage counseling, Post Traumatic Stress Disorder (PTSD), blended family issues, Critical Incident Stress Management (CISM), death notification, addictions and addictive behavior.

Someone once said that there is a unified diversity in the triune God – a plurality in oneness. God is one being in three persons – all of whom are diverse, but not separate.

Such must be the theology of a chaplain. The chaplain serves one God – who is plural in nature, Father, Son and Holy Spirit – but he/she must be diverse in subject matter but not separate from the God they represent.

Marketplace Theology Includes

Breaking outside the religious box and realizing that the mission field is not only in some foreign country but there is a mission field which includes chaplaincy within the community better known as the marketplace. These include police chaplains, fire/rescue chaplains, hospital chaplains, hospice chaplains and corporate chaplaincy. All of these areas of ministry in the marketplace requires specialized training and experience.

Part of the strategy of the church must be to develop a vision and instill that vision within the called *"ministers"*(Ephesians 4:1) and that they are assigned to the marketplace which includes: business, government, education, media, religion, arts, entertainment and the family.

There is a difference between someone who is called to be a minister and someone who is called to be a missionary. A minister is someone who has been <u>called</u> to the marketplace. A missionary is someone who has been <u>sent</u> to the marketplace on a specific mission. Whether a person is called or sent they must understand that God has placed them in that position and that position is not to be seen as a job. It is the responsibility of the Church to teach, train, empower, commission and affirm the individual minister that where they are serving in the community is their ministry.

If we look in scripture we see that Jesus modeled this concept. He chose twelve small business owners, trained them and then sent them back into the marketplace for ministry. His teaching and training covered marketplace missions. He did not speak about church life but rather instructed those business owner's that they could do what He did. He was concerned about the impact that they would have on the community. His very life validated marketplace missions in that he ministered healing to everyone He met.

Marketplace Missions Strategy

Strategic planning will challenge the status quo and help design and execute better systems designed to minister in the marketplace. Ministers in the marketplace know that their strategic plans require constant monitoring of reviews and updates.

When strategic planning is in place it should cause the individual minister to experience the best return on time, energy and resources. Strategic planning will help identify corporate values and people will see the connection between their assignment in the marketplace and their vision.

Strategic planning will help each individual minister develop long term goals and short term objectives and how to achieve them. To appreciate what Jesus intended for the church to do in marketplace missions we must look at the difference between the Twelve and the Seventy.

The Twelve wanted to change the temple system and restore the Kingdom back to Israel. The Seventy was assigned to change the world by establishing Kingdom influence and principles through marketplace missions. The Twelve wanted to send the crowds away, build tabernacles, call fire down if necessary just to keep Jesus for their selfish ambitions. Jesus overruled all their petty issues and called the Seventy to model for the Twelve what He really wanted in the marketplace.

Jesus called his twelve disciples to him and gave them authority to drive out impure spirits and to heal every disease and sickness.

These are the names of the twelve apostles: first, Simon (who is called Peter) and his brother Andrew; James son of Zebedee, and his brother John; Philip and Bartholomew; Thomas and Matthew the tax collector; James son of Alphaeus, and Thaddaeus; Simon the Zealot and Judas Iscariot, who betrayed him.

These twelve Jesus sent out with the following instructions: "Do not go among the Gentiles or enter any town of the Samaritans. Go rather to the lost sheep of Israel. As you go, proclaim this message: 'The kingdom of heaven has come near.' Heal the sick, raise the dead, cleanse those who have leprosy drive out demons. Freely you have received; freely give.

"Do not get any gold or silver or copper to take with you in your belts— no bag for the journey or extra shirt or sandals or a staff, for the worker is worth his keep. Whatever town or village you enter, search there for some worthy person and stay at their house until you leave. As you enter the home, give it your greeting. If the home is deserving, let your peace rest on it; if it is not, let your peace return to you. If anyone will not welcome you or listen to your words, leave that home or town and shake the dust off your feet. Truly I tell you, it will be more bearable for Sodom and Gomorrah on the day of judgment than for that town.

"I am sending you out like sheep among wolves. Therefore be as shrewd as snakes and as innocent as doves. (Matthew 10:1-16; Luke 10:1-23) NIV

The Mission of the Church

The Church has been sent to change the world by establishing Kingdom influence in seven areas which include religion, family, government, education, business, arts, and media. The church must be mission minded with people who have been called into the marketplace to establish the Kingdom through the ministry of chaplaincy. Jesus referred to the Church twice but the Kingdom was mentioned 136 times. The Church is the ecclesia or the "called out ones" (Romans 8:30).

God knew what he was doing from the very beginning. He decided from the outset to shape the lives of those who love him along the same lines as the life of his Son. The Son stands first in the line of humanity he restored. We see the original and intended shape of our lives there in him. After God made that decision of what his children should be like, he followed it up by calling people by name. After he called them by name, he set them on a solid basis with himself. And then, after getting them established, he stayed with them to the end, gloriously completing what he had begun.

The mission of the church is to extend the influence and principles of the Kingdom to every nation (Matthew 28:18, 19). The best way to accomplish the purpose of missions is through marketplace ministers reaching into the community. This subject was addressed by Jesus in Matthew 5:13 -16 (Message Translation).

Let me tell you why you are here. You're here to be salt-seasoning that brings out the God-flavors of this earth. If you lose your saltiness, how will people taste godliness? You've lost your usefulness and will end up in the garbage.

Here's another way to put it: You're here to be light, bringing out the God-colors in the world. God is not a secret to be kept. We're going public with this, as public

as a city on a hill. If I make you light-bearers, you don't think I'm going to hide you under a bucket, do you? I'm putting you on a light stand. Now that I've put you there on a hilltop, on a light stand—shine! Keep open house; be generous with your lives. By opening up to others, you'll prompt people to open up with God, this generous Father in heaven.

If the Church does not infiltrate the territory of the enemy and defeat the enemy on his ground (the marketplace), he will attack the Church on her turf (church meetings). God never intended the marketplace to belong to the enemy. There were many "power encounters" in the book of Acts that sets the parameters for marketplace missions.

Life as a chaplain is not a theater with a script; it is a gathered community that lives by divine life with the assignment to invade the local community in order for the community to be influenced by the church.

Two

.

WHERE IT ALL BEGAN

Some twenty plus years ago I was pastoring and towards the end of our mid-week service a deputy sheriff, who I knew, slipped into the congregation and waited until I had finished with the closing prayer. At the end of the prayer he came up to me and asked if I could help him with a sensitive issue. I went with the deputy to the home of an elderly gentleman who had passed away from natural causes and the deputy needed my help informing the family that their loved one had passed. It was a difficult situation in that I did not know any of the family and there was so much grief and anguish not only in their faces but in their spirit as they faced the passing of their loved one.

It was at that time that I realized the importance of ministering to families in similar situations in the future. I began a long and eventful journey reading and studying everything I could in regards to ministering to people outside the church in every situation.

The more I made myself available to the sheriff's department the more I was in demand. Yet at this time there were not many so called "chaplains" in the area nor was the ministry of "chaplaincy" heard of. There were hospital chaplains and a few hospice chaplains but not law enforcement chaplains. There were a few fire/rescue chaplains but not many across the United States.

In my studies of becoming a chaplain I was made aware of the intricate details and immediate needs for a chaplain to serve within the law enforcement community. Officers needed a chaplain just like the families who had lost a loved one. However the preparation to become a law enforcement chaplain demanded understanding the culture of how a law enforcement department thinks and lives. Police officers are trained professionals and because of the nature of their training they need someone that they can call a confidant or friend and who is a professional as well.

One of the unique challenges a law enforcement chaplain faces is breaching the "Blue Wall." There seems to be a social wall that is intentionally erected and judiciously guarded by the officer from the outside world. Only the accepted can enter and many times that does not included the officer's wife and family. The chaplain only gains entry when he or she demonstrates a consistent time of commitment, a nonjudgmental posture in all questionable circumstances, an affirming attitude when criticism is the usual response, a demonstrated interest in the life and concerns of the officer and his or her family, and genuine acceptance of the officer in spite of differences, fallibilities, and expectations.

Troop 9 Foxtrot was an independent group, far from headquarters and dependent upon one another for support. Today the new chaplain was assigned to a trooper who would introduce her to the territory. Twenty minutes into the ride and some juicy gossip about the troop, the trooper claimed an emergency, and dropped off the chaplain at an intersection to be picked up by another trooper. After a similar experience, she as picked up by yet another trooper.

Two rides later, a sergeant passing noticed the chaplain standing at a rural intersection. After hearing a quick explanation, the sergeant laughed and asked, "It was a test. They want to know if they can trust you to keep a secret and if you'll complain when it gets uncomfortable or inconvenient."

Consistency of presence, complete honesty in all matters, and true humility, which is known as servanthood, will be what earns the trust, confidence, and respect necessary for meaning relationships and effective ministry inside the "Blue Wall".

A person that feels that they have been called to serve as a chaplain cannot get into the front seat with a police officer and set the boundaries that the officer must respect him and his sanctified holy office. That is the first thing that will turn a police officer off! Remember I said that police officers have a culture of their own? To be able to minister to a police officer a chaplain must learn to respect the boundaries and territories of that officer while in his patrol car. That is his office where he carries on business for the police department. His office has his/her computer, charger cords, radio, snacks, drinks and sometimes a spit cup for his tobacco juice. His trunk is usually equipped with tactical gear along with papers and files. There will also be jackets and wind breakers in case he runs into inclement weather.

This atmosphere is much different than the pastor's office. Everything in the pastor's office is in order and the pastor's library is arranged the way he likes it. There is no smoke in the air, no trash on the floor, no empty drink cups and all the necessary cords are hid under the pastor's desk. Those who come to see the pastor are usually his parishioners and they are there for a specific purpose and usually only the pastor can meet that specific purpose or need with counsel, prayer and a kind heart.

The one major difference between a pastor and a chaplain is the pastor has been trained to talk, and the chaplain has been trained to listen. The pastor can control the direction of the discussion but a chaplain must learn to listen and follow the direction of the discussion.

The law enforcement officer must always be listening to his radio and when he gets a call he knows that he is entering the unknown and must be alert and be vigilant to make an assessment the situation quickly so that he or others don't get hurt. A hand shake never settles the problem and usually those he is responding to are angry and hostile and he knows that he must present the professional side of his training whether he likes it or not. Words that are exchanged usually are not pleasantries but can be curse words and words of anger and it is the job of the officer to get control of the situation as soon as possible. Even then sometimes the officer is forced to take the individual to jail.

A chaplain will find himself standing by the patrol car watching and observing as the officer and the backup units handle calls. Specialized training lets the chaplain know that during the peak of the call is the time to be listening and praying for the officers. There have been times when I was with an officer and we were called to a doctor's office where an individual had a heart attack and the patient was in need of medical attention. While the medics and fire fighters administered CPR I stood back and prayed. Later I was asked by the officer why I didn't try to get close to the patient to pray and my response was that "the effectual fervent prayer of a righteous man availeth much" (James 5:16). My prayers are just as powerful standing back as they would be touching the patient besides; my ministry is a ministry of "presence".

Many pastors would fail the test here because they think that it is their place as a minister to extend healing to the patient when the primary concern of the patient is medical care

Briefings

Briefing to a police officer not only is where he/she receive instructions from his/her supervisor but it is where corrections are made in report writing and special assignments are made for that shift. Briefing is also where officer's bond with each other. Sometimes their jokes are off color and they treat one another like brothers and sisters. This is what we call a "police family" or the :Blue Wall". A chaplain has to earn the right to be accepted into the family. Many times the lieutenant or sergeant will not recognize the chaplain and his/her spiritual role and the chaplain cannot become irritated or show resentment. The chaplain's purpose is to be a "ministry of presence" which means seen and not heard.

It took me years to come to understand the quirky personalities of each police officer yet I wanted so much to be able to get inside their click and join their world so that I could minister to them. When the supervisor asked "who wants a chaplain to ride with you" many times no one responded and that is the ultimate rejection for a minister. Everyone loves the chaplain and we have all the answers to their problems. Yet that is not how it goes down in law enforcement.

It is important for the chaplain to arrive early at the police department and circulate the halls saying hello to all the employees. The chaplain needs to make him/her known to the lieutenant or sergeant and ask them if he/she can ride with his shift. Remember, the police department or fire/rescue station is not the chaplains church building. When you enter their territory it can be lonely and discouraging because as chaplain you have not broken through the wall of resistance that is held by the culture of those in uniform.

One of the rewarding things is that after you get through all the quirky personalities and all the bonding issues and you finally get out on the road you realize the professionalism of the officer. The training that he/she went through in the academy and the continued training which is what makes these officers so special. They are professionals within their industry and we need to respect them as so.

The Culture of Chaplaincy

What makes a chaplain successful in law enforcement or fire/rescue is not only his training but the ability to walk away from his church and put on the hat of chaplaincy and then patiently realize that he may be accepted or rejected. As the officer's look at the chaplain they ask questions with their eyes like, "if I let you ride with me can you leave all that religious stuff behind"? "Can you forget anything that you might see or hear tonight that will destroy my career"? "Can you handle my cursing or handle my lighting up of one cigarette after another"? "If something goes wrong tonight can I depend on you staying out of my way"? "Can I trust that you as a chaplain are not going to bore me with all your religious rhetoric and that you are not going to try to get me 'saved'"? "If I share my feelings about my department can I trust that you want say anything to my superiors?" Every chaplain has to learn to be tough yet tender because there will come a day when those officer's will begin asking you questions and sharing intimate details of their lives. The chaplain must learn that everything that is said to him/her is in confidence and there is no minister's meeting where the chaplain can buddy up to his friends and tell all the war stories. There are no discussions of church sizes or what are you doing to create growth. Being a chaplain means walking a path of loneliness until you meet other chaplains who you can confide in. Yet the ministry of chaplaincy is the most rewarding and exciting ministry in the marketplace.

I remember riding with an office the night our military troops stormed Dessert Storm. The officer didn't want me in his car yet he took me as a courtesy to the lieutenant. The atmosphere was cold and the climate was stiff which prevented any communication. Three hours went by as we rode through the city and sitting at a red light around 11:30 pm he erupted with the following question: "Do you think that this war, Dessert Storm, could be the beginning of the end? Do you think this could lead to the battle of Armageddon?"

Wow, what a way to break the ice and get to know one another. Yet I was praying under my breath that the Lord would allow me to minister to him before the night was over. Minister, did I ever! For the next 2 hours we discussed this issue and at the end of our theological discussion I asked if I could pray for him. He pulled the patrol car over and I prayed.

We ended up at another officer's house, a friend of the office I was riding with, who was dying with cancer. As we entered the house I felt led to encourage him to go and be with his friend and I would keep the officer's wife in the kitchen. She was needing ministry and a friend to talk to.

In a few minutes we heard someone praying and the wife and I looked around the corner and the officer that I was riding with had his friend on his knees praying for his salvation and his healing. What a picture! I learned from this experience that you never know what the Lord is going to do and when we think nothing is happening, something is happening.

It took me several years to gain the trust and confidence of one or two officers that were willing to accept me and realize that I represented a "ministry of presence". I didn't see anything, I didn't hear anything, and I didn't say anything. They knew that I had earned their confidence by just being their friend. With no discussions of religion or anything to do with religion I was just an individual willing to ride to gain their trust, be their friend and help wherever I was asked to help. Then there came that break in the door when a death notification had to be made and most police officers hate to deliver death notices. The way people react to the notification and the need to comfort the recipient of the bad news was not in their training manual and they for sure do not know how to deal with the spiritual aspect of the families and their religious beliefs. Now that is where I was able to stand up and become that "ministry of presence" that would assist the officer and the department and at the end the family would always thank the department but not the chaplain. Chaplaincy is a ministry of being a servant to both the police family and to the community in a time of need with very little recognition if any.

The cultures of both police work and fire/rescue demand tolerance and perseverance on the part of the chaplain. Many times the chaplain will ride for hours without any calls but then there will be other times when the chaplain will barely get his breathe.

Chaplains have to learn that when officers want to talk to other officer's or they are called into the lieutenants office, the chaplain needs to find another place to be because communication is part of the way first responders build their culture and community. Many times their culture will be closed off to outsiders. This is not a personal statement to the chaplain, only a mechanism that they use to guarantee security for their culture and their job.

Training

There are many different agencies that provide good and efficient training for chaplains. As a law enforcement chaplain one of the best organizations to belong to is The International Conference of Police Chaplains (ICPC). They have been in existence long enough and involved with different police agencies across the United States and other countries to develop some of the best training curriculum around. Law enforcement chaplains are encouraged to join ICPC and as the chaplain fulfills their curriculum requirements they have different levels of membership. When putting an individual on as a police chaplain many law enforcement agencies recognize and endorse chaplains who are members of and who have been trained by ICPC.

A chaplain should request that their police department make training a part of the yearly budget. The department should and must see the chaplain as a professional trained to do the work of the ministry within the department which requires yearly training updates.

Chaplains who serve in fire/rescue departments are encouraged to look into The International Federation of Fire Chaplains (FOFC). They have developed outstanding curriculum as well. Again, many departments look to see if the individual who will be serving as chaplain is a member and if they have certifications from either FOFC or ICPC.

Another outstanding agency that produces in depth studies for the chaplain is The International Critical Stress Foundation (ICISF). The courses that a chaplain can take through ICISF are more specialized and will be a great asset in working with people in crisis.

Any chaplain serving in any department would be beneficial to look into taking all courses that the Federal Emergency Management Association (FEMA) offers on-line. All these courses are free and it helps to magnify how the government works and how all local, state, and federal departments are to function in the event of a major disaster.

It is good for all chaplains to seek out the Emergency Management (EM) director in their county and get to know him/her well. Learn to be present and make yourself available to the director and all the departments within your county that cooperate with Emergency Management.

Three

The Power of Presence

"If lips and life do not agree, the testimony will not amount to much."

— Harry Ironside

Hours became days as the family waited for news of their elementary-age autistic boy who had disappeared in a rural community. The child had been left in the care of his teenage sister and unbeknownst to her, he had slipped out the bedroom window. A volunteer chaplain had been working tirelessly on the search and rescue team. The search went all through the night, and the next morning the searchers found the remains of the little boy floating in a nearby pond.

The chaplain, joined by another chaplain, proceeded to the home of the family to tell them that the body of their son had been found and that he was dead. After the family was notified, the chaplain understood the importance of linking the family with a local support system. The chaplain asked if the family attended a local church and the family gave the name of the pastor where they attended. The chaplain told the pastor what had happened and said that the family had requested for him to come to their home and pray with them. The pastor told the chaplain that he was fairly new to the congregation and that he didn't know the family. The chaplain stressed the urgency of the situation and the emotional state of the family and then told the pastor again that the family had requested his presence. The pastors response was, "I don't know the family and I am not coming".

When the chaplain told the family what the response of their pastor was what do you think was their response? What message did this pastor send to the grieving family? What message did this send to the volunteers who had searched tirelessly, giving their time to help a family that they did not know who was in need? What did this say about the church in that community?

Working with hurting and grieving individuals can be messy. In order to be affective as a chaplain there are times when you will have to get into the trenches with and get dirty.

That is what happened when I was called by a motor officer in our city to accompany him to the home of a family whose sister was killed in a head on collision. Once the family saw the officer in uniform and me in uniform they knew that we were there with some bad news. They just didn't know what the news was about.

As the officer and I entered the residence we both noticed that there was about 2 inches of water all over the floor. Every room had water coming from somewhere in the house. So it was evident that we were in the trenches on this one. You also have to realize that there were many members of the family already in the home including small children who were playing in the water as well as climbing all over the furniture.

It came time for us to tell the family and when I shared the news of the death of their loved one the sister slid down the wall into the water. It didn't take anytime for her clothes to become soaked with the water, and no one knew where the water came from. To complete my ministry that evening I had to kneel down beside the sister and minister to her during her time of grief as well as to the other members of the family.

The question that we must ask ourselves as chaplains is who will stop in the face of human suffering to give their time and resources to someone in need? Often there is no reward, no acknowledgement, no media present to record the good deed.

Personal Risks

A chaplain had been serving for months providing emotional and spiritual care after the aftermath of a disaster. The chaplain called his incident command leader and expressed, "I am worried and a little scared because something happened to me today that I have never experienced." The chaplain went on the say that he was sitting with a person listening as the person poured out his heart about all that he had lost. The chaplain said, "I was sitting there listening to him and thinking, I just don't care anymore."

There are two critical things that effective and well trained chaplains do to sustain themselves for the long haul. Chaplains must set boundaries and understand their limitations. Sometimes chaplains, being men and women of God, feel that they are the only one who can help another person. When this thought occurs, it should be a signal that you need to fortify your boundaries. Chaplains who are efficient and want to remain effective must have an outlet to process and dump their emotional baggage from helping others, as well as having a well-established way of refueling emotionally, physically, relationally, and spiritually.

In Mark 6:30-34 (NIV), Jesus wanted to spend time with His disciples in a "solitary place", but the crowd was demanding more of their time and attention, and they had been so busy that they didn't even have time to eat. When the boat with Jesus and His disciples arrived at the "solitary place" Jesus had compassion on the crowd and He began teaching many things.

It is good when chaplains can team up with other chaplains to work together especially in disaster situations. In Mark 6:7 and Luke 10:1 Jesus sent His disciples out in pairs.

*Calling the Twelve to him, he began to send them out two by two and gave them authority over impure spirits. (*Mark 6:7) NIV

After this the Lord appointed seventy-two others and sent them two by two ahead of him to every town and place where he was about to go. (Luke 10:1) NIV

Teaming up with another chaplain can be good for several reasons. When you co-minister with another chaplain you can draw strength and wisdom from the other person. Also, each chaplain brings their own unique style, and if you are paired up with someone who compliments your ministry style, you can make up for the other's weakness.

Not only is there the potential of physical risks but there can be emotional risks as well. Often chaplains will feel remorse or regret because they can't do more than what they are already doing. The very nature of following Christ compels us to take action for those who are hurting, and yet we have to balance our own ministry to others with caring for ourselves, our spouses, and our children. Many times it is the one's we love most who suffer the greatest because as chaplains we feel we must take care of everyone else. It is critical for chaplains to carefully assess their motivation as to why they are serving. Do we serve because of the adrenaline rush we get from the lights and sirens, or do we serve because we have been called to the hurting, grieving, and wounded?

Working with grieving and hurting individuals can be a messy business. True ministry of presence is getting in the trenches with those who are hurting and extending yourself as a spiritual caregiver. A common sign of burnout is when chaplains just don't care anymore.

Chaplains who serve alongside law enforcement or fire/rescue must learn that they represent Christ in the form of a "ministry of presence." What that means is that the chaplain doesn't represent his church or denomination. Simply put, a ministry of presence is primarily about *being* rather than *doing*. The chaplain represents Christ and must be ready to respond to any situation when called upon as a "representative" of Christ, not the Church. A ministry of presence is about the "art of being". Jesus was a master at the heart of being. He clearly knew who he was and what he was all about. He moved with purposefulness when faced with all kinds of adversity and crisis situations.

Look at how he handled the women caught in adultery in John 8:4. There is something about this story that chaplains would do well to emulate. Though Jesus took action, there was something about his presence that brought great relief and peace to the women.

Through experience, the chaplain needs to ask the individual he is ministering to if they have a church family. If they do, then it is the responsibility of the chaplain to call their pastor and invite him to the scene and then step back and allow the pastor to take over the intimate ministry of that family or individual. During a crisis situation every family needs their own spiritual support system which may not include the chaplain.

Jennifer Cisney and Kevin Ellers says that chaplaincy is organic in its construction; relational in its functioning; scriptural in its form; Christ-centered in its operation; Trinitarian in its shape; communitarian in its lifestyle; non-elitist in its attitude; and non-sectarian in its expression.

This "ministry of presence" is one of the hardest things to learn when dealing with first responders. Chaplaincy is so closely related to pastoral ministry that it is hard for the individual chaplain to not be used in every situation. Yet every situation that the chaplain goes to is different and requires a different response and ministry. Sometimes the chaplain is dealing with children sometimes youth and sometimes adults. There will also be times when the chaplain will be dealing with all three.

T. Austun-Sparks identifies the "organic" church with the following statement: "God's way and law of fullness is that of organic life. In the Divine order, life produces its own organism, whether it be vegetable, animal, human or spiritual. This means that everything comes from the inside. Function, order and faith issue from this law within. It was solely on this principle that we have in the New Testament came into being. Organized Christianity has entirely reversed this order."

The church as we read about in the New Testament was "organic". By that I mean it was born from and sustained by spiritual life instead of constructed by human institutions, controlled by human hierarchy, shaped by lifeless rituals, and held together by religious programs.

What Is at the Core of the Ministry of Presence?

Once we as chaplains realize what survivors really need, it takes away the pressure to perform. The "ministry of presence" is best defined as *being fully with another person, exhibiting a non-anxious, comfortable presence while demonstrating "God with us" through the interconnectedness of the human interaction. When people are in crisis and hurting, they really crave the safe, comforting presence of others.*

An effective ministry of presence provides

- a comforting and non-anxious presence of someone who can empathize with their situation.
- It also creates a safe environment without any outside threats or distractions.
- It allows the victim to be emotionally and spiritually present in that very moment of need.
- It demonstrates a "I will be with you" through this event.
- It demands creative and good listening skills on the part of the chaplain.
- It requires that the chaplain is focused on others rather than self-focused.
- It requires an attitude of acceptance and not a judgmental attitude.
- It requires a servant's heart in order to meet basic needs of the individual.
- It requires good thinking skills to help victims and survivors sort through the task at hand.

When the chaplain shows up on a scene, and there are people who are traumatized and in crisis, you visibly demonstrate God's presence in a tangible way. You become symbolic of His hands, His feet, and His arms of security and strength. You are an extension of the church.

As chaplains we need to ask ourselves, is ministry always presence and is presence always ministry? Just because you are on the scene physically does not mean that you are on the scene spiritually. Your ministry is not presence if you are not wanted there. Chaplains must learn to read the non-verbal cues that people give. The sheriff's department here in our county is proud of their chaplains, 25 or so, and when an accident occurs they let other chaplains know that their chaplains will take care of the situation, whatever it may be.

Many times police officers in the department where I serve as chaplain will ask people who are in crisis if they want a chaplain and many times those people say no. As chaplain I cannot get offended at that response. Some people just want to be left alone during their time of sorrow and grief.

Another way to be present is through the power of prayer. That is why it is so important that when people are going through difficult situations that they solicit others to pray with them.

Confess your faults one to another, and pray one for another, that ye may be healed. The effectual fervent prayer of a righteous man availeth much. (James 5:17 (NKJV)

Here in our county we have some 58 chaplains just in law enforcement and fire/rescue, and that does not include the hospital chaplains, or hospice chaplains. One of the things that we are trying to do is to network together and get to know one another so that when a disaster or event occurs we will know each other ahead of time. We also submit prayer requests to the other chaplains asking for their prayer as we serve in our community.

Accidents

A ministry of presence is also recognized when a trained chaplain is called to an accident or to the death of an individual and sometimes the chaplain can do nothing but stand on the side and watch and pray. Fire/rescue personnel do not need a chaplain in their way when they are trying to extricate people from vehicles. Paramedics do not need the chaplain interfering with their patients while they are administering medical attention. They only have so much time to "package" up the patient and get them to the hospital. Minutes matter!

Fire/rescue chaplains do not have the gear nor do they have the expertise to assist in those events so it is mandatory for the chaplain to stand back and observe what is going on. However the chaplain is a professional and all the emergency personnel really like it when the chaplain is standing on the side praying for them. Remember, the chaplain can become emotionally affected by the things he/she is looking at just like the first responders. It is better for the chaplain not to become contaminated by the scene if possible. Contamination can cause the chaplain to need professional defusing or debriefing by the Critical

Incident Stress Management Team if what the chaplain see's begins to affect him. Standing far enough away that the events of what is happening does not affect the individual chaplain is essential and important.

Chaplains know that they are never to get out at an accident scene without having their emergency vest on. This vest identifies the chaplain as part of the "first responder" team. This vest should be issued by the department and the chaplain should have it with him every time he rides. Again it is important that the chaplain have such rapport with the officer that the officer doesn't have to worry about the chaplain.

The chaplain needs to know who the Battalion Chief is or who the lead investigator is on a scene. The chaplain must check in with that person so that everyone knows that the chaplain is on the scene along with the other emergency personnel.

As chaplain when I arrive on any scene after everyone is finished and they are wrapping up their gear I go around asking each emergency personnel how they are doing. Chaplains must remember that emergency personnel are one of their own and the chaplain must show care and attention to those who were involved in the rescue.

By-standers

When I arrive at an accident scene I look around to see if there are any by-standers who have been affected by what they have experienced in witnessing the accident. Many times those who arrive first have begun CPR or are offering aid to those who have been injured.

In February of 2016 another chaplain and myself were called to the scene of a head on collision where there were ten (10) individuals laying on the ground in trauma. Because we were delayed in getting to the scene the sheriff's department had one of their chaplains present and he had been ministering to the by-standers. What he ran into was that the by-standers were the first people on the scene and one of the by-standers was doing CPR on an 18 month old, who died, while other by-standers were helping other patients until the emergency crews arrived. The sheriff's department chaplain had his hands full working with those by-standers and the crisis that they were having.

It is through specialized training, years of experience that the chaplain learns when to involve other chaplains such as hospital chaplains, hospice chaplains or chaplains from another law enforcement agencies.. Chaplains are not all-inclusive! That means that we are not out in the field to be the only chaplain to serve in the situation. There will be times when a chaplain will need to call chaplains from other agencies to assist in the scenario. This is why chaplains must learn to network with each other so that they feel comfortable with those who serve in the same capacity.

When a chaplain becomes accustomed to serving and knows his/her authority in the Lord they realize that they do not have to touch or lay hands on patients or victims as their denominations may teach. Their very presence is a healing measure.

Protocols

Chaplains need to know the protocols of their department as well as other departments within the community. Every chaplain should be required to read the Standard Operating Procedures Manual (SOP's) of the department that they are serving with. By reading the SOP's the chaplain will have a better understanding of how the department in general operates and these instructions will better enhance the understanding of the department.

It is important when doing a ride-a-long that all emergency personnel who maybe responding understand that you are not going to get in their way while they are carrying out emergency procedures.

This is one of those places where chaplains can lose respect and confidence with law enforcement officers real easily. It is not about you! It is about serving the immediate situation, whether it is through the officer or the emergency personnel on the scene.

When a department initiates a chaplaincy program that program must be under someone who on the administrative level. Law enforcement agencies are structured like a military unit therefore everyone has a chain-of-command and they must not violate that authority. Chaplains are no different in that there is someone within the structure that the chaplains report to.

More Training

As time went along I became familiar with organizations such as The International Conference of Police Chaplains (ICPC) and through my relationship with them I began to broaden my understanding of police chaplaincy through specialized training.

In attending their training classes I also met some tremendous individuals that helped mold my understanding of the ministry of chaplaincy and I picked up some great input from those who were more experienced than I was. I made it a weekly part of my schedule to ride with a police officer. My ride-a-longs went from a couple of hours to complete shifts. When I was in another city for training I asked for permission to do a ride-a-long with that department and I compared departmental procedures with the department I was serving.

I learned that every police department had a set of Standard Operating Procedures and I needed to read them to understand why the officer's made decisions the way they did. The SOP's are the police officers Bible.

As time went along the ministry of chaplaincy began to grow and more and more police departments were putting chaplains on to serve their department. The more chaplains that came along the more training was demanded.

I made friends with the Director of the Police Academy in my county and before long he asked me to take the teacher's training course so that I could teach the new recruits in each academy class. That led up to my being asked to attend the Advanced Chaplain's Training offered by the FBI in Quantico, Virginia.

Department Etiquette

If you're going to be a successful chaplain within your department you will need to learn to meet everyone in the department. Meet the janitor, secretaries, and different office personnel all the way up to the Chief of Police or Sheriff. Everyone in that department has a name and they need to know that you care for them not just the officer. As department chaplain you are spiritually responsible for all personnel their families and their needs. You need to meet all the detectives, special units such as Critical Response Team (CRT), swat team members, explorers and any volunteers that the department might have.

Remember, the department knows who you are and many times they will exercise their carnal instincts to discourage you and make you feel like a heel. They will speak with a crude language and it will sound like they don't respect you but as chaplain you must learn that much of this is their individual coping mechanism and the way they talk is how they survive the stress of the job.

Members of the department will suffer marital conflict, separations, and sometimes divorce. Personnel have children that can create unbearable home life situations which creates stress for the employee and they should find your presence comforting and spiritually uplifting. But many times as department chaplain you will find yourself being asked to listen to their problems to see if you can assist them in their time of pain.

Post Traumatic Stress Syndrome is a growing problem among law enforcement agencies and as chaplain you need to have some training as to how to discern the symptoms of PTSD which is becoming a problem with many officers. As chaplain you should be educating and exposing the department to the need for intervention and care.

One of the characteristics of law enforcement agencies is that they think that the individual officer should learn to deal with his/her stress personally and suck up their emotions so that it doesn't affect their work. Though that is admiral, the problem is that the individual will eventually begin to feel the results of not dealing with the emotion and the long term affect can become destructive behavior, addictions, and other symptomatic behaviors.

Four

*"The kingdom of God does not consist in talk, but in power,
that is, in works and practice. God loves the 'doers of the word'
in faith and love, and not the 'mere hearers,' who, like parrots
have learned to utter certain expressions with readiness."*

— *Martin Luther*

The desire to be a chaplain begins with intentional preparation for spiritual care ministry such as seminary education, specific training in counseling and leadership, integration of life experiences. The chaplain is commissioned and committed to proclaim God's love to a world that may never step into a church service. As a minister of differing cultures, interests, and religions, the chaplain becomes a pluralist, seeking multiple ways to allow people to express their faith or lack of faith in meaningful ways being exclusive without compromising his or her own faith.

A chaplain lives in the tension of seeking to find balance between serving God, serving people, and serving the department that employees him; between his accountability to the ecclesiastical body that endorsed him and to the department that retains his services.

The Church must reject non-biblical assumptions that separate the clergy from the laity and learn to resist the widespread damaging effects of this separation. The need is to challenge the tendency to see ministry and missions as part of the work of paid ministers and missionaries who are a percentage of the whole body of Christ.

Every believer must accept and affirm their own personal ministry and mission as functioning wherever they are at in the marketplace. Pastors and church leaders must support marketplace ministers in the community and the workplace.

The church must develop effective training systems that will equip God's people in complete discipleship, which means to live, think, work, and speak from a biblical view point with missions as the central topic – effectiveness in every place or circumstance of daily life and work.

Christians, known as ministers (Ephesians 4:1) are in skills, trades businesses and professions that are able to go in places where the average traditional leader cannot go which means that they have no presence or influence. Marketplace ministers must be valued as an aspect of the ministry of the local church.

Jesus gave instructions to the church through His great commission. He said;

"Therefore go and make disciples of all nations, baptizing them in the name of the Father and of the Son and of the Holy Spirit, and teaching them to obey everything I have commanded you…"(Matthew 28:19) NIV

Many individuals within the local church are being commissioned to "go" out from the local church into the community to minister the gospel of Jesus Christ. I believe that is why we are seeing such a surge in the number of individuals who are being trained in the field of "first responders". In order to have a better understanding of what we are being called to do we need to understand what Jesus meant in Romans 12:1-2.

"Therefore, I urge you, brothers, in view of God's mercy, to offer your bodies as living sacrifices, holy and pleasing to God – this is your spiritual act of worship. Do not conform any longer to the pattern of this world, but be transformed by the renewing of your mind. Then you will be able to test and approve what God's will is – his good, pleasing and perfect will".

Five

WHAT MAKES A GREAT CHAPLAIN?

To be called by God to serve as a chaplain is quiet an honor. This calling is not to be taken lightly and it requires the individual to search his/her heart for true sincerity. Since most volunteer chaplains are from local churches within the community it is not advisable for a lead pastor of a local church to serve. The reason for that is the pastor has a congregation and that congregation is the pastor's primary concern. Since the pastor has no idea when and if he is going to get called out it is hard for the lead pastor to give the time necessary to the chaplains program. It is better for an associate pastor, a lay pastor or a retired minister to serve in that capacity.

The individual that is going to serve must have an endorsement from his/her congregation or denomination and must be in good standing with that body of believers. The individual that is planning to serve as chaplain must go through a rigorous back ground check along with extensive interviews with a chaplain's board.

The department that he/she is going to serve is his/her congregation. Rather than ministering from behind a pulpit the pulpit becomes the front seat of a patrol car. The reputation and character of the chaplain must be held on the same level as the local pastor. The department will eventually see the chaplain as their pastor.

Spiritual Strength

The individual that is going to serve as chaplain must be a born again believer and must have his/her spiritual foundation in the Word. They don't have to be a theologian but they must have knowledge of the Bible and how to apply the Word in everyday circumstances.

A chaplain cannot project himself as a "Bible thumping" preacher. Remember that the ministry of the chaplain is a "ministry of presence". He/she is the representation of the God that we serve and that the individual must be prepared to minister God to whoever needs Him. The chaplain must also remember that he/she is not to proselytize people. The work of the chaplain is not to get people to attend their church but to get people to see God as their source for their immediate need.

Chaplains will find times when they can refer an individual to a local church but it must be at the discretion of the individual that the chaplain is ministering to. This is also true for those individuals who have been trained as "first responders" by their denomination to serve when a disaster o

Understanding Your Department

The process in becoming a chaplain within a department can be slow and frustrating. The individual applying for chaplaincy must fill out a detailed application provided by the department of which he is going to serve. After the application is completed the department will take finger prints of the candidate. After the finger prints have been cleared then the department will do an extensive background check. This is where the process slows down because the background check can take several months.

Once a person has been selected to serve as chaplain with a department that chaplain should be notified by the department that he/she will be sworn in at a swearing in ceremony just like a sworn officer. During the swearing in ceremony it is important that the department recognize and officially introduce that chaplain to the department. By swearing in the chaplain and officially recognizing him it lets all the officers and personnel know that the chaplain has an official position with the department. It is also important that the department issue the chaplain an official uniform and badge. The chaplain should also be issued an official ID number just like the officer's.

It is from that moment that the chaplain must learn and understand the culture of that particular department. There are protocols on the way things are done. The chaplain must understand that departments of law enforcement follow a military protocol. There is rank and file and everyone obeys those who have authority over them. Not only do they obey those over them but the chaplain must learn who he/she is responsible to and that is their contact person for everything that they do.

Life in the ministry is much different than life in the police department. In the ministry pastor's have a tendency to get there when they want to. They like to sleep as late as they want to. As a chaplain whenever you are called out, during the day or in the early morning hours, those who called you are expecting you to get there as soon as possible. Chaplains do not have lights and sirens so you must learn to drive responsible and safely.

To be an effective chaplain the individual should endeavor to take courses that will give him/her a better understanding of what they are doing as a chaplain. Training is offered on a regular basis and every opportunity should be made to take as many courses as possible. Many courses that are offered are free such as FEMA courses 100 thru 700.

Once you are on a scene don't expect to leave soon. Sometimes the nature of the investigation will require you to present and available for many hours. Sometimes you will start on a particular scene but you may end up across town in someone's home delivering a death message or meeting a family at the hospital to console them in the loss of a loved one. You must know what the protocol of the hospital chaplains is and try your best to work within that protocol. That is why it is important to network with the hospital chaplains and get to know their standard operating procedures.

As chaplain you must know what the city policy is for insurance coverage. Though you are a volunteer you are covered under the departments insurance in case of injury or death.

You need to know that while you are on a ride-a-long you are covered under the departments insurance. Anytime that you are called or you are making a visit to the department on department business you are covered under their insurance. That is why every police department needs to give the chaplain an employee number and a radio so that you can let dispatch know that you are 10-8 (on duty) for the department enroute to wherever they have called you.

If the department asks you to hold a Bible study on a regular basis as chaplain you need to know that it is legal and permissible as long as every employee agrees to attend on their lunch hour and they sign a paper stating that they are voluntarily attending the Bible study on their lunch hour. Remember, part of your specialized training is knowing what the law say in the event the department wants you to teach the employees.

As chaplain make yourself available for special occasions and events. Do a ride-a-long in the Christmas parade or participate with the department in handing out Christmas presents to under privileged kids in the city. Be sure to visit all personnel on a regular basis.

Understanding Other Departments

Good and effective chaplains will attend meetings of other agencies as well as other departments within the community. Most communities have what is known as Emergency Management Agency. Get to know the director of Emergency Management. This person can be a real asset to your chaplains program and as chaplain you can make yourself available to the county.

Many times departments within the community will have round-table disaster scenarios that the chaplain can set in on and learn how the county works during the event of a disaster.

All chaplains must learn that in the event of a disaster within their community there is a proper protocol in checking in to the scene and getting recognized by the command staff. Whenever a disaster occurs and volunteers are needed there is a location where all volunteers check into the scene. Chaplains should not just show up on the scene and begin to serve without first being recognized.

Once a command center is set up the command center then identifies the volunteers that they need to be on that scene. When the needs are identified by the Command the chaplain may not be doing what he has trained to do. He may be passing out water, or helping victims go to a rescue center. Whatever the need chaplains must be willing to serve.

Six

THE EMOTIONAL PART

"Bitterness imprisons life; love releases it."

— *HARRY EMERSON FOSDICK*

Individuals who serve as chaplains must be individuals who have emotional stability, flexibility in crisis, and a broad base of ministry skills. They must be a calm presence and demonstrate quite confidence. It is a well known fact that *people won't care how much you know until they know how much you care.* They must be well founded in their theological belief system and have a balanced understanding of the Bible. This is one of the attributes that we look for when choosing chaplains. Not everyone is capable of serving as a chaplain because of the nature and atmosphere that the chaplain has to participate in. This includes the atmosphere around the department, the personnel and when called out to minister at a scene.

People who want to be chaplains must be aware that they may get called to some gruesome scene in the middle of the night and they must be capable of handling what they see. If the chaplain is on a ride-a-long with a police officer that unit may get called to an accident where there maybe multiple victims who are injured and requires immediate medical attention. Because the chaplain is on the scene he/she will experience tremendous emotional trauma by what they see, hear, smell and witness. This is much different than serving in the security of a church. The chaplain may feel that they are a strong individual but like all first responding chaplains they may need time out as well.

It was the last of the winter season here in Central Florida my wife and I were spending some time together watching television. My phone rang and the Chief of Police in our city was calling me to see if I could respond to a multiple shooting in our city where 3 young men had been shot, 2 had died and the third had survived. Upon arrival at the scene the Chief asked if I would minister to a 12 year old girl who had witnessed her dad shoot these 3 men. The little girl was traumatized and very upset at what she had seen. After a brief interview I told the Chief that we needed to call a mental health person to work with the girl because of her level of being traumatized.

I walked through the scene checking with every officer and noticed that several were showing signs of distress and anxiety. Their distress and anxiety was not about the shooting as such but they were mad and perplexed that the father had shot these men in front of his daughter and that she had witnessed such a brutal crime at such a young age.

While on the scene I found myself helping the officer's put up road blocks to preserve the crime scene. I also found myself assisting neighbor's who had known the family and they were feeling anxious concerning the gravity of the crime. There was blood everywhere, not just inside the apartment where the crime occurred, but there was blood on the shooter, and his daughter and down the steps of their apartment. This was a crime that the girl should never have been involved in nor shoud she have witnessed such a horrific crime. There was also a blood trail down the street where one of the victims had crawled to spare his life.

In the early hours of the next morning the lead detective asked me to ac-company him to the family homes of the two victims who had died to deliver death notifications. We also had to go to the third victims home to let that family know that their son had been shot but had survived and that he was in the hospital.

Delivering death notifications is another emotional event because when you wake family members up at 2:00 am to tell them a family member has been killed the reaction you receive is mixed and conflicting. Yet there is no greater ministry of presence than to be present and embrace family members during their time of sorrow, grief and anger.

These notifications cannot be carried out in a quick or hastily time frame. The chaplain must network the family members with other family members as well as call their minister to come and be part of their support mechanism. Calling people in the middle of the night requires them to get dressed and drive the distance to where you are at. Many times they aren't awake yet and they haven't had their first cup of coffee yet.

I shared this real life story with you to let you know that after a night like this was, and the sun has come up it might be good to network with other chaplains for support and to help you through your moment of anxiety. Networking with other chaplains is a good way to establish a means to counter the emotional times when you feel like you can't take anymore. Chaplains will experience the same emotional burn-out that fire/rescue personnel experience and it will require the chaplain to step back and ask for support and counseling. This is especially true when first responder chaplains respond to infant traumas such as drowning, death caused by an accident, or other related calls.

The family members of chaplains must also realize and prepare for the moment when the chaplain has had enough and the family must look for the signs that their loved one needs some attention.

Law enforcement and fire/rescue employees are familiar with Critical Incident Stress Management (CISM) in which first responders can go for defusing or debriefing. This is an important event in the welfare and mental health of the first responder as well as the chaplain. Sometimes the chaplain serves as part of the CISM Team but other times he will need to be part of those who are defused or debriefed.

Critical Incident

A "critical incident" is any incident that causes an individual to experience unusually strong emotional reactions which have the potential to interfere with the individual's coping ability to function. These can be large scale events, such as terrorist attacks, hurricanes, floods, school shootings, and such. An automobile accident, a suicide, or a house fire are also critical incidents and can affect the individuals and families directly.

A critical incident (the actual event) can often be confused with the crisis (a person's adverse reaction to the event). *As a chaplain, it is critical that you tailor your response to the reaction of the event rather than to the event itself.* This is so important because if you only respond to the event rather than to the crisis, then you may focus your attention on individuals who may not be having a crisis or who are mildly affected while you bypass others who may be severely affected and in need of immediate attention.

An example of this distinction can be seen in the following story. A group of college students were attending a school sporting event. Because their team was losing badly at half time they decided that rather than staying for the remainder of the game they would go back to their room shared by two of the women in the group. When the group of six students arrived at the apartment, they walked in on a young man who had broken into the apartment. Because he was unarmed when he was interrupted by the six young women, he picked up a kitchen knife and grabbed one of the girls, who was standing closet to him. Holding the knife to her throat, he threatened to kill her if he was not allowed to leave the apartment safely. As he backed slowly towards the door, he held the knife to her throat while continuing to threaten her friends that if they made one move toward him he would slit her throat. Once out the door he pushed his victim down and fled the scene.

A crisis response team was put together and after much questioning one of the members could not understand how the young lady who was held with a knife to her throat was not more upset. After questioning her she admitted that the moment the young man grabbed her and placed the knife to her throat she began to pray and through her prayers she had a calm that the young man was not going to hurt her. The Holy Spirit gave her a peace that prevented her from experiencing a level of fear that would be normal for such a situation.

One of the other roommates did not have the same reaction to the event. While the crisis response team was focused on the young lady who had the knife held to her throat this other young lady was experiencing a psychological crisis significantly more intense than that of any of the other students. This young lady began to express agitation, anxiety and her symptoms would begin to manifest in the next few days. She had trouble focusing, inability to sleep, lack of appetite and occasional crying spells.

Because the crisis response team only focused on the young lady who had a knife held to her throat they missed the trauma of the other women involved in the same situation.

Simply put, what happens is the individual has a normal reaction to an abnormal situation. Even though the incident is over, and several days have passed, the individual chaplain may experience some strong emotional or physical reactions. It is very common, and in fact very normal, for people to experience emotional aftershocks (posttraumatic stress) or what we call "critical incident stress". Posttraumatic stress is a natural and adaptive part of human functioning. This is Gods "alarm system" which helps us survive life-threatening situations. This is what we call "fight" or "flight" response. When we are faced with danger or a situation that our brain interprets as dangerous, our bodies undergo a number of psychological and chemical changes. These changes help us "flee" the situation or "fight off" the danger.

The intrusiveness of traumatic events can be so invasive that they may seem to temporarily take control of one's life. Survivors may find that they are washed back and forth between reliving the trauma, and being overwhelmed by floods of intense emotion., impulsive action, intrusive thoughts, involuntary physiological responses, and numbness and immobilization.

Sometimes these aftershocks (stress reactions) appear immediately at the scene, or sometimes they appear a few hours or days later. In some cases, weeks or months may pass before the individual shows any kind of physiological reaction. There can be triggers that cause the chaplain to begin to relate back to the traumatic event that caused great emotional pain.

I'm reminded of the family who was out shopping for Christmas during the Thanksgiving holidays. They had shopped in another town and they shopped until the stores closed. While driving home they took a country road that would make their trip home faster. Because of being tired and exhausted from shopping the entire family was asleep except the father who was driving.

Because of the lateness of the evening, and the unfamiliar roads, the dad accidently ran a stop sign and t-boned a semi-truck. Firefighters and paramedics worked tirelessly extricating everyone from the car.

The next day as chaplain I was checking on the crew and they were all fine the night before but now there was new anger, especially on the medics part because the news media had reported in the morning paper that if the family had had their seat belts on the family would possibly have been spared. The medics were angry because they were the ones who had to cut each seat belt to get everyone out of the car, yet the news media was not there. This article from the news media "triggered" a crisis from the medic crew.

When an individual experiences these stress reactions it is not an indication that they are crazy or losing their mind. It simply indicates that the particular event was just too powerful for the person to manage by themselves.

If a chaplain serves as a lead pastor within the community he/she must recognize that they cannot carry this emotional baggage into the pulpit with them. Everything must remain confidential! Listed below are several stress coping strategies that chaplains need to observe.

Stress Coping Strategies

Appropriate physical exercise along with proper relaxation
Stay busy
Don't allow normal reactions to make you feel crazy
Find someone to talk to
Don't numb the pain with drugs or alcohol
Stay active and reach out to people
Maintain a normal schedule as much as possible
Find someone to workout with
Give yourself time to feel rotten
Keep a journal – write your way through sleepless nights
Do what feels good to you
Realize that those around you are under stress

Don't make any major life changes

Make daily decisions which will help restore control over your life

Get plenty of rest and drink plenty of liquids

Dreams and flashbacks are normal – don't fight them – they will decrease over time

Eat well balanced and regular meals even if you don't feel like it

Family and Friends

Learn to listen

Spend time with the traumatized person

Offer your assistance and a listening ear and be sure to listen for help

Reassure the individual that they are safe

Help with everyday tasks like cleaning, cooking, caring for family members, and take care of children

Give the individual private time

Don't take their anger or other feelings personally

Don't say things like; "it could have been worse," or "I know what you are going through". Traumatized people need your support and encouragement not your empathy

Are You a Safe Person?

It was Friday evening and I was called by dispatch to go to a certain address where one of our medic units had been dispatched to the drowning of a child. These types of calls are also hard on all first responder units.

The story as I was told was that a young family was not paying attention to their youngest child, 5 years of age, and the child had wandered outside the house. When the parents realized that the child was quiet they began to search every room of the house as well as outside.

The home was neatly tucked into some wooded area so the sheriff's department along with fire/rescue was searching the woods. Everyone had over looked the in ground pool located right by the back door. While everyone was looking in the woods someone finally suggested that the fire department pump all the water out of the pool thinking the child might be in the water. The pool water was dark green and covered with algae. One fire fighter decided to get a pole off the truck and drag the bottom of the pool to see if the child was there. It wasn't too long until reality had set in and everyone knew that the child had drown when the fire fighter pulled the limp body from the water.

When I arrived on the scene the ambulance had already left for the hospital with the child. Because I wasn't needed on the scene any longer I was asked by the Battalion Chief to go to the station of the medic unit and wait for them to arrive to see if I could assist the EMT who was having a hard time dealing with this call.

When the medic unit arrived at the station the EMT grabbed my neck, began hugging me, crying and saying that he wanted to quit. After spending time with the crew I found out that this trauma alert call had been his 4th call and every child had died due to drowning.

Being a safe person is absolutely critical when working with people in crisis. One of the important things that help people feel safe is confidentiality. As chaplain you must provide an environment so safe that the person who has been traumatized is able to release their pain, fear, anger, sadness, and depression – whatever he/she is feeling. But they also need to be able to tell their story and experience their emotions with a person who will allow them to express themselves without judgment, fear, or denial. Further, they need a person who will not try to fix them but rather will feel comfortable in the presence of their pain.

Scriptures on Hope

Being a chaplain means that the ministry you perform is outside the pulpit and outside the local church. The department that you serve becomes your church and your rewards will be based on how well trained you are as well as the experience that you bring to the department as a chaplain. I have taken the liberty to share some scriptures with you that you will find helpful as you begin your journey as a chaplain or if you are already a chaplain.

Psalm 42:5 (NIV)

Why are you downcast, O my soul? Why so disturbed within me? Put your hope in God, for I will yet praise him.

Psalm 33:16-22 (NKJV)

No king is saved by the multitude of an army; A mighty man is not delivered by great strength. A horse is a vain hope for safety; Neither shall it deliver any by its great strength.

Behold, the eye of the LORD is on those who fear Him, On those who hope in His mercy,

To deliver their soul from death, And to keep them alive in famine.

Our soul waits for the LORD; He is our help and our shield. For our heart shall rejoice in Him, Because we have trusted in His holy name.

Let Your mercy, O LORD, be upon us, Just as we hope in You.

Psalm 131:1-3 (Message)

GOD, I'm not trying to rule the roost, I don't want to be king of the mountain.

I haven't meddled where I have no business or fantasized grandiose plans.

I've kept my feet on the ground, I've cultivated a quiet heart.

Like a baby content in its mother's arms, my soul is a baby content.

Wait, Israel, for GOD. Wait with hope. Hope now; hope always!

Psalm 130:5 (NIV)

I wait for the Lord, my soul waits, And in His word I put my hope.

Psalm 25:3 (Message)

I've thrown in my lot with you; You won't embarrass me, will you?

Or let my enemies get the best of me? Don't embarrass any of us

Who went out on a limb for you. It's the traitors who should be humiliated

I Corinthians 13:7

[Love] always protects, always trusts, always hopes, always perseveres.

1 Timothy 1:1 (NIV)

Paul, an apostle of Jesus Christ by the command of God our Savior and of Christ Jesus our hope.

Romans 5:1-5 (Message)

By entering through faith into what God has always wanted to do for us—set us right with him, make us fit for him—we have it all together with God because of our Master Jesus. And that's not all: We throw open our doors to God and discover at the same moment that he has already thrown open his door to us. We find ourselves standing where we always hoped we might stand—out in the wide open spaces of God's grace and glory, standing tall and shouting our praise.

There's more to come: We continue to shout our praise even when we're hemmed in with troubles, because we know how troubles can develop passionate patience in us, and how that patience in turn forges the tempered steel of virtue, keeping us alert for whatever God will do next. In alert expectancy such as this, we're never left feeling shortchanged. Quite the contrary—we can't round up enough containers to hold everything God generously pours into our lives through the Holy Spirit!

2 Corinthians 1:7 (NIV)

And our hope for you is firm, because we know that just as you share in our sufferings, so also you share in our comfort.

Jeremiah 14:8 (NIV)

O Hope of Israel, its Savior in times of distress, why are you like a stranger in the land,

Like a traveler who stays only a night?

Seven

"When by the malice of enemies God's people are brought to greatest straits, there is deliverance near to be sent from God unto them."—

DAVID DICKERSON

It was Saturday evening and church had just let out when I received a notice on my telephone that there had been a bad accident in the Northeast part of our county. When I arrived home the coordinator of the Polk County Critical Incident Stress Management Team was calling me to inform me of the accident. I was dispatched to the scene along with another chaplain and it took us about 20 minutes to arrive on scene. Because of the location of the accident we had to stop and walk through the scene to let the Command Staff know that we were present.

Our purpose in being dispatched was to check on all the fire/rescue personnel and make sure that they were all handling the situation ok. This was a multiple casualty accident and there were 10 trauma alert patients in which all of them had to be taken to the hospital in the next city. 10 ambulances, two fire trucks, training officer, along with the Deputy County Manager, and multiple by-standers.

As the chaplain and I got out of my car I said to him that we needed to stay focused on the command staff and not look to our right or left or we could become contaminated by the scene and would need to go through debriefing as well.

After the command staff arrived on scene he made the initial assessment and he assigned one of our paramedics as a triage medic. There was an 18 month old that had passed away on the scene and as the triage medic was making her calls to the other medic units the mother of the 18 month old was hysterical and demanding that the medics continue to try to save her baby. After every patient was transported to the hospital, we felt that due to the nature of the call all of the medic units needed to be taken out of service for debriefing.

When the units arrived at the station we found that there were several EMT's and paramedics that were having a difficult time because several of the EMT's had small children at home themselves. Since every patient was a trauma alert the triage medic was having a difficult time because she could not get the helicopters to fly because of inclement weather and she had to hear the cry of the mother who had lost her 18 month old on at the scene. Several of the trauma alerts were children and a second child died on the way to the hospital.

Pain and suffering are not new to our society. We find many instances throughout the Bible where pain and suffering are mentioned. In Genesis 4:10 we see where cries of lament rise from the ground with the blood of Abel, and God takes notice and intervenes. In Psalm 103:6 David says that God cares for a suffering humanity. Therefore we can conclude that there is a cycle of loss, pain, adversity, and death from which no one is spared. A gentleman by the name of Powlison (2006) says," Often the biggest problem for any sufferer is not the 'problem.' It is the spiritual challenge the problem presents" God's grace and your suffering".

Triage

It is common for law enforcement, paramedics, and firefighters to arrive on a scene where multiple injuries have occurred and the patients are waiting for someone to help them. One of the first things emergency crews do when they arrive on a scene is to assess the situation and the Commander appoints one of the paramedics to perform triage to ensure that they first provide medical care to the people who need it the most. Failure to triage the patients can be deadly!

Triage is difficult because the medic cannot listen to the patients, they must package the patient and transport based on the assessment at the scene. The chaplain has to be careful not to get emotionally involved if he is on the scene because chaplains are not part of the medical team and we do not understand the protocols for triage.

When there is a serious accident with multiple casualties it is important for the chaplain to check on all law enforcement and fire/rescue personnel to see if any of them are showing that they are having a crisis. Many times checking with the Command Staff first will help because the Command Staff is also watching the crew on the scene.

Critical Incidents/Crisis

Without proper training many chaplains will make a common mistake when arriving on a scene and identify the particular, distressfully negative incident as a crisis. This can lead the chaplain to falsely assume that there is a state of crisis which may not be true. A crisis occurs when a stressful incident overwhelms an individual's ability to cope effectively in the face of a perceived challenge or threat (Everly & Mitchell). Therefore, a survivor may experience a critical incident and yet never truly enter a state of crisis.

A response to an event may be defined as a crisis when:

1. psychological homeostasis (balance) has been disrupted;
2. one's usual coping mechanisms have fail to reestablish homeostasis; and
3. the distress engendered by the crisis has yielded some evidence of functional impairment (Caplan, 1961, 1964; Everly & Mitchell, 1999).

Two phychologist by the name of Lawrenz and Green (1995) indicate that the following factors influence the stressful impact of an event:

1. The anticipation or experience of physical or psychological pain.
2. The experience of life changes (the more numerous the changes, the greater the stress).

3. The cumulative amount of stressors in ones life.
4. Social support, such as friends and family (the less the support, the greater the perceived stress).
5. Potential coping options or resources (the fewer the options or resources, the greater the perceived stress).
6. Ambiguity or sadness of the event.
7. The emotional and physical characteristics and present state of the individual.

Common Reactions following a Traumatic Event

Even though individuals react differently to different traumatic events clinical researchers have identified a common pattern of behavioral, biological, psychological, spiritual, and social responses. Chaplains must recognize these reactions are normal reactions:

Physical Effects

- Fatigue, exhaustion
- Increased physical pain
- Sleep disturbances
- Cardiovascular strain
- Reduced immune response
- Change in appetite
- Decreased libido
- Hyper arousal
- Nausea
- Dizziness
- Headaches
- Gastrointestinal problems
- Increased startle response
- Muscle tremors
- Profuse sweating

- Digestive problems
- Somatic complaints
- Ritualistic behavior
- More accident prone
- *Emotional Effects*
- Shock
- Fear/terror
- Irritability
- Anger
- Grief or sadness
- Depression
- Depression
- Despair
- Loss of pleasure from familiar activities
- Nervousness
- Blame
- Guilt
- Emotional numbing
- Helplessness
- Identification with the victim
- Difficulty feeling happy

Interpersonal Effects

- Increased relational conflict
- Reduced relational intimacy
- Impaired work performance
- Impaired school performance
- Feeling abandoned/rejected
- Alienation
- Decreased satisfaction
- Distrust
- Externalization of blame

- Externalization of vulnerability
- Over protectiveness

Cognitive Effects

- Impaired concentration
- Impaired decision-making ability
- Memory impairment
- Disbelief
- Confusion
- Distortion
- Self-blame
- Decreased self-esteem
- Decreased self-efficacy
- Worry
- Dissociation (e.g., tunnel vision, or dreamlike or "spacey" feeling)

Spiritual Effects

- Spiritual disconnection from God
- Questioning God and theological beliefs
- Anger at God
- Spiritual emptiness
- Withdrawal from the faith community
- Increased awareness of mortality
- Guilt for feelings, e.g., anger, desire for vengeance)

Eight

"It is wonderful what miracles God works in wills that are utterly surrendered to Him. He turns hard things into easy, and bitter things into sweet. It is not that He puts easy things in the place of the hard, but He actually changes the hard thing into an easy one."

— HANNAH WHITALL SMITH

- It is possible to be present physically but not emotionally. Don't get distracted.
- Remember that as a chaplain you must be completely present with those you are going to minister to. Be in prayer on the way to the scene and ask God to give you the right words to say.
- Understand that just being there as a minister of "presence" is more powerful than anything else that you can do.
- Being a minister of "presence" means that you are representing God and the Godhead.
- Be observant and realize when there is nonverbal language and know when it is time to go.
- Be sure to surround the victims with a strong support group before you leave, such as family, neighbors, and church.

Meeting Safety Needs

- Remember that law enforcement, and fire/rescue personnel are all vulnerable during an event. This includes command staff as well.
- Personnel sometimes are likely to have a reduced level of functioning and a diminished capacity to make good decisions to protect themselves and others.
- Make sure bystanders feel safe and do whatever you can to assure them of that safety.
- Make sure that all who are involved in the incident are also surrounded by people who are safe.
- Educate those support groups on how to keep personnel safe.

Making Clear Assessments

- Assess the basic needs of the personnel on scene and take whatever steps necessary to help meet those needs.
- Leave assessing physical damage to law enforcement and fire/rescue.
- Assess traumatic elements to which the first responders may have been exposed.
- Assess the personnel's perception about the critical incident. Is it a critical incident or is it just a stressor?
- Assess the available resources and make them available to all who need them.
- Assess the personal impact to the personnel.
- Don't assume anything concerning long-term impacts. Check up on your personnel after the event is over.
- Look for ways to foster resiliency and help the personnel sustain emotional and spiritual growth through the adversity.
- Asses the social support system and take steps to connect everyone to a good support system.
- Assess how you can educate your department as to what signs and symptoms to watch for and how to help staff and personnel cope in any situation.

Making Practical Care Assessments

- You must know your personnel and let them know they can ask for help.
- Be present to serve, not to be served.
- Remember that emergency personnel may be overwhelmed by the critical incident and need more support, help, and direction than normal.
- Don't do things for your personnel that they can do for themselves. Wait to see if they are going to need your help.
- When you make an assessment don't assume that you know what the personnel is going to need.
- The care you present should be practical and meet the basic needs.
- Understand that the "ministry of presence" may be all that the personnel needs. Sometimes that includes just being with the other crew members.
- Don't interfere with the natural coping mechanism.
- Make sure you have permission from your Command Staff as well as your personnel to help them.

Providing Information

- Make sure you have correct and clear information on what happened, who was involved, how many were involved and get the location of the event.
- As you make an assessment be sure to listen to every detail of your personnel.
- Make sure your personnel has up-to-date resource material.
- Be sure your personnel can get in contact with you.

References

Bilezikian, Gilbert. Community 101. Grand Rapids, MI: Zondervan, 1997

Caplan, G. (1961). *An approach to community mental health.* New York: Grune and Stratton

Cisney, Jennifer S. & Ellers, Kevin L. *The First 48 Hours, Spiritual Caregivers as First Responders,* Nashville, TN: Abingdon Press. (Pg 40, 41, 42)

Ellers, K. L. (2008). *Critical Incident Stress Management: Emotional and spiritual are in disasters.* Elliott City, MD: International Critical Incident Stress Foundation.

Everly, G. S., Jr., and Mitchell, J. T. (1999). *Critical incident stress management* (2nd ed.). Elliot City, MD: Chevron Publishing Co.

Kennedy, John W. *Secret of His Purpose.* Bombay: Gospel Literature Service, 1963

Lawrenz, M. and green, D. R. (1995). *Life after grief: How to survive loss and trauma.* Grand Rapids, MI: Baker books.

Powlison, D. (2006). *God's grace and your suffering in Piper,* John and Taylor, John, *Suffering and the sovereignty of God. Wheaton, IL: Crossway Books*

Appendix A

Professional Organizations

American Association of Christian Counselors (AACC)

PO Box 739
Forest, VA 24551
(800)526-8673
(434)525-9480 Fax
www.AACC.net

American Association of Pastoral Pastoral Counselors (AAPC)

9504 A Lee Hwy
Fairfax, VA 22031
(703)385-6967
(703)352-7725 Fax
www.aapc.org

American Correctional Chaplains Association (ACCA)

Box 422
East Lyme, CT 06333
(860)691-6549
(860)739-9375 fAX
www.correctionalchaplains.org

Association for Clinical Education (ACPE)

1549 Clairmont Rd., Ste 103
Decatur, GA 30033-4635
(404)320-1472
(404)320-0849 Fax
ww.ACPE.edu

Canadian **Association for Pastoral Practice & Education (CAPPE)**

7960 ST. Margaret's Rd
Ingramport, NS B3Z 3Z7
Canada
(866)442-2773
(902)820-3087 Fax

College of Pastoral Supervision & Psychology (CPSP)

PO Box 162
432 W. 47th St, 2W
Times Square Station
New York, NY 10108
(212)246-6410
(212)305-5666 Fax
www.cpsp.org

Council on Ministries in Specialized the Training (COMISS)

PO Box 2409
Poquoson, VA 23662
(757)728-3180
(707)929-7388 Fax
www.comissnetwork.org

National Association of Catholic Chaplains (NACC)

PO Box 070473
Milwaukee, WI 53207-0473
(414)483-4898
(414)483-6712 Fax
www.nacc.org

National Association of Jewish Chaplains (NAJC)

901 Route 10
Whippany, NJ 07981-1156
(973)929-3168
(973)736-9193 Fax
www.najc.org

National Conference on Ministry to Armed Forces (NCMAF)

7708 Griffin Pond Ct.
Springfield, VA 22153
(703)455-7908
(703)455-7948 Fax
www.ncmaf.org

**International Conference of
Police Chaplains (ICPC)**

PO Box 5590
Destin, FL 32540-5590
(850)654-9736
(850)654-9742 Fax
icpc@icpc, gccoxmail.com

New York Board of Rabbis (NYBR)
Chaplaincy **Commission**

136 E. 39th St., 4th Floor
New York, NY 10016-0914
(212)983-3521
(212)983-3531 Fax
www.nybr.org

**National Institute of Business &
Industrial Chaplaincy (NIBIC)**

1770 St. James Place, Ste 550
Houston, TX 77056
(713)266-2456
(713)266-0845 Fax
www.nibic.org

Appendix B

To see a full list of all religious endorsing bodies contact:

The National Conference on Ministry to the Armed Forces (NCMAF) & Endorsers Conference for Veterans Affairs Chaplaincy

4141 N. Henderson Rd., Ste 13 / Arlington, VA 22203
(703)455-7908
(703)276-7948 Fax
Email: jack@ncmaf.org or Maureen@ncmaf.org

Alliance Baptist
www.allianceofbaptist.org

American Baptist Chaplaincy & Pastoral Counseling Services
www.abc-cpcs.org

Apostolic Catholic Orthodox Church
www.apostoliccatholic.ag.org

Church of Christ
chaplaincoc@worldnet.att.net

Church of God (Anderson, Indiana)
www.chog.org

Churches of God, General Council
Paparson@aol.com

Assemblies of God, General
Council of
www.chaplaincy.org

Baptist General Convention of
Texas
www.bgct.org/TexasBaptist

Christian Church (Disciples of
Christ)
www.disciples.org
dthompson@dhm.disiples.org

.

Christian Church of North
America Christ Fellowship
Church
www.spirit-filled.org

Christian Reformed Church in
North America
www.crcna.org/chaplaincy

National Baptist Convention USA,
Inc.
Drcthomas1@cs.com

National Jewish Welfare Board/
Jewish Chaplains Council
www.jcca.org

Church of Jesus Christ of Latter
Day Saints (LDS)
clawsonfw@ldschurch.org

Church of the Nazarene
djennings@nazarene.org

Coalition of Spirit-Filled
Churches (CSC) Also:
International Ministerial
Fellowship, Christian Church
of North America, Christ's
Fellowship
www.spirit-filled.org

Conservative Baptist
Association of America (CBA)
www.cbcchaplains.net

Conservative Baptist Fellowship
www.cbfnet.org

Episcopal Church Endorsement
Office of the Bishop of
Chaplains
www.ecusa-chaplain.org

Evangelical Church Alliance
(ECA)
www.ecainternational.org

The Evangelical Covenant Church
www.covchurch.org/ministry

Pentecostal Church of God, Inc.
lmboyles@aol.com

Evangelical Free Church of
America
www.efca.org/chaplains

Presbyterian Council for
Chaplains & Military Personnel
(PC)
www.erols.com/pccmp and
www.pcusa.org

Evangelical Lutheran Church of
America (ELCA)
www.elca.org/chaplains

Presbyterian & Reformed Joint
Commission on Chaplains and
Military Personnel (PRJC)
www.pcanet.org

The Full Gospel Churches Also:
The Association of Vineyard
Churches
www.chaplaincyfullgospel.org

Progressive National Baptist
Convention, Inc.
BobnJacki@juno.com

Islamic Society of North America
www.siss.edu

Reformed Church in America
(RCA)
www.rca.org

Lutheran Church-Missouri Synod
www.lcms.org/spm

National Association of
Evangelicals (NAE)
www.nae.net

National Association of Catholic
Chaplains
www.nacc.org

National Baptist Convention of
America, Inc.
jwdaile@aol.com

Regular Baptist Churches, General Association of
www.garbc.org

Roman Catholic Church
jroque@milarch.org

Seventh-day Adventists US, General Conference of
www.adventistschaplains.org

Southern Baptist Convention North American Mission Board
www.namb.net/chaplain

United Church of Christ
www.ucc.org

United Methodist Church General Board of Higher Education and Ministry
www.gbbem.org/chaplains

United Pentecostal Church International
www.upci.org or www.ugst.org

World Council of Independent Christian Churches
www.wcicc.org

Suggested Reading and Resources for Law Enforcement Chaplains

Beyond the Badge, A Spiritual Survival Guide for Copes and Their Families; Charles Ferrara, Lieutenant, N.Y. P. D. (ret)

Chaplaincy in Law Enforcement (What It Is and How To Do It); DeRevere, Cunningham, Mobley, and Price, Authors; Charles C. Thomas, Publisher

Cop Shock, Surviving Post Traumatic Stress Disorder PTSD; Allen R. Kates

Crisis Counseling, A Practical Guide for Pastors, Counselors and Friends; H. Norman Wright

Death Notification, A Practical Guide to the Process; R. Moroni Leash

Devotions and Prayers for Police Officers; Steven J. Voris

Emotional Survival for Law Enforcement; Kevin Gilmartin

Grieving a Suicide: A Loved One's Search for Comfort, Answers, and Hope; Albert Y. Hsu

Handbook for Chaplains, Comfort My People; Mary M. Toole

How to Be a Perfect Stranger, The Essential Religious Etiquette Handbook; Stuart M. Martins and Arthur J. Magida

Law Enforcement Funeral Manual; Chaplain William Sanders

Lives Behind the Badge; Kristi Neace

Ripples of Suicide: Reasons for Living; Harold Elliott

Spiritual Survival for Law Enforcement; Cary A. Friedman

Standing Courageous: Kristi Neace

The Empty Chair: The Journey of Grief After Suicide; Beryl S. Glover and Glenda Stansbury

The Perfect Stranger's Guide to Funerals and Grieving Practices; Stuart M. Matlins

Building King's Beloved Community: Foundations for Pastoral Care and Counseling with the Oppressed. Chinula, Donald M., Cleveland, OH: United Church Press, 1997.

Critical Incident Stress Management. Everly, George, and Jeff Mitchell. 2nd ed. Elliott City: Chevron 1999

Compassion Fatigue. Figley, Charles. Elliott City: Chevron, 1994

I Love a Cop: What Police Families Need to Know. Kirschman, Ellen. New York: The Guilford Press, 2000

Ethics and Spiritual Care: A Guide for Pastors, Chaplains, and Spiritual Directors. Labcqz, Karen. Nashville: Abington, 2000

Disaster Relief Training Manual. Paget, Naomi. Alpharetta, GA: North American Mission Board of the Southern Baptist Convention, 2004

Suggested Reading and Resources for Fire/Rescue Chaplains

<u>The Fireman's Wife</u>; Susan Farren

<u>Marriage Under Fire</u>; Dr. James Dobson

<u>Life Resurrected – Extraordinary Miracles Through Ordinary People</u>; Jessie Birkey

<u>Your Shield and Buckler</u>; Jorge Diaz

<u>Sirens For The Cross – Inspirational Stories of On-Scene Fire and Rescue Calls</u>; Tommy Neiman with Sue Reynolds

<u>Living With Grief and Sudden Loss – Suicide, Homicide, Accident, Heart Attack, Stroke</u>; Hospice Foundation of America

<u>The First 48 Hours – Spiritual Caregiver as First Responders</u>; Jennifer S. Cisney and Kevin L. Ellers

<u>I Love a Firefighter – What the Family Needs to Know</u>; Ellen Kirschman, PhD

Leadership Secrets of Colin Powel; Oren Harari

Federation of Fire Chaplains Training Manual, http://www.firechaplains.org

Trauma and Recovery. Lewis-Herman, Judith. New York: Basic Books, 1992

Made in the USA
Lexington, KY
10 May 2017